I0542016

Arcadia Found

The Art
of Being
in
Community

ISBN 979-8-218-05080-1

Typesetting and layout by Walter Cheatham & Peter Norman
Set in Traditional Arabic

Cover: *The Course of Empire: The Arcadian or Pastoral State* by Thomas Cole 1834

Cover Design by Deanna Cheatham

Arcadia Rising Press

Dedicated to
Deanna, Summerlea, and Bee

The deepest gratitude
to Peter Norman,
without whom this reality
would still be just
an idea.

Arcadics is the praxis of investigating, manifesting, and realizing an Arcadian Ontology requiring a deep, critical examination of the fundament of human existence; wholly exploring the middle ground between the rational and the emotional, the primal and the modern, between atomism and holism, human and Nature: a conduit into that space between shared by both human and non-human; poetically generating the wisdom of home-making towards a reunion of humanity with Being.

Finding Arcadia

Arcadia Found

I'm going to tell you a story:

a transformative experience

in an economy of breath

Please get comfortable

allow yourself to settle in

relax your hands

your toes

open your ears

open

your Mind

but most importantly

open your Heart

This is not a story about ecological

agriculture,

it's about our relationship

with each other

      and the rest of existence

it's about our future

and whether or not we'll have one

I mean
some days I haven't the heart to even look
it in the face...to see it all.
Some days
...I just bury my head in the sand
...others I am a crusader, hell bent on
rescuing humanity from itself,
not an eco-warrior,
not an anthro-warrior,
an onto-warrior!
...but...
my battle cry falls on deaf ears
drowning
in the cacophonous whirring of machines
churning human flesh into pixels,
feeding the inanimate.
I have to cover my eyes
so I don't see it:
Being
dripping
from the bloody gaping maw
of Artifice.

My dear fellow *Homo sapiens,*

What.

Are.

We.

Doing?

Our technological successes and scientific-

method–glimpsed visions of the fabric of

existence have left us fool-hardy and smug,

doggedly clutching the pervasive,

pernicious, pestilential belief that we have a

fingernail's hold on objective reality.

Us?!

A species with access to only three paltry electromagnetic colors, a scant few audible frequencies, no claws, no fangs, and physiologically finicky offspring. That we think we have half a bleeding clue about how Mother Nature should do things…well, aren't we just overachieving taxonomic upstarts. And hypocrites! Western civilization is consuming entire genera of endangereds, forests echo with the melodious chorus of chainsaws drowning the silent screams of old growth who remember Buddha as a prince, Socrates a soldier and baby Jesus in cloth diapers. It is a gargantuan, self-serving, dictatorial, corporate mega-beast ruling our every waking nanosecond. Souls, tarnished by greed, worship a theocracy of positivist science, sacrificing those who live in the wrong tax bracket, at the wrong latitude on the altar of two-day shipping, steering a cancerous civilization right into the very viscera of our ailing planet asking for more,

more,

MORE!

Dancing to the incessant, bleating ministrations of monotonal media megalopolies broadcasting neuron-degrading, contradictory, thirty-second soundbites of " *We* know, *they* don't!" Violent protests against viral narratives that thrive on violence flood the streets.

While wildfires compete with torrential floods for carbon-choked airtime and rising seawaters turn to acid, a dualistic environmentalist body bids humans to live less, do less, be less from behind ramparts of delusional do-gooding—perched atop shaky higher ground all the while complicit in a pandemic of paradigmatic contagion.

This dominant paradigm of decomposing epistemology desperately grasping with gnarled, arthritic fingers at what remains of its intellectual hegemony should be taken out back of the barn and shot.

Poverty, Famine, Misery, and Squalor persist in even the most affluent societies of Western Culture, a culture too deeply engrossed in the ceaseless scroll of smartphone screens, chasing the fool's errand of unbridled growth, marching to the fossil-fueled drumbeat of progress right out of kinship with each other and the rest of existence—a species of pixelated automatons whose continued membership in the community of life

is no longer guaranteed.

But…

I once stood on a farm, and I'm going back

Because the human species is a species

threatened by habitat loss,

and I'm a human…one might say I have a

vested interest.

You're human, as well…

so, let's say you have a vested interest, too.

I once stood on a farm, and I'm going back

Because there I saw Nature leaping over

fences to hear crickets serenade tomatoes

lounging under the branches of peach trees.

There, not every apple goes into the basket,

but stays on the limb, a loft apartment for a

family of worms who return a portion of

their earnings to the roots,

an offering of gratitude.

There, the paradox of the one and the

many balances

between blackberry bushes

and the chicken coop.

There, life and death tip their hats to each

other each morning in passing.

There, waste eliminates want and the garter

snake in the grass eats its own tail.

Today, the pig puts yesterday in one end

and tomorrow comes out the other.

There, Being is being one…

…with itself.

I once stood on a farm, and I'm going back.

Because I saw a living allegory.

Because there, before me, was a time after

humans remember what community is.

I witnessed past and future collide.

I saw it and thought,

"If they could only see...what I see."

I once stood on a farm, and I'm going back.

Because after I was there, I wondered.

I once stood on a farm, and I'm going back.

Because there, peaceful revolution grows

next to the rosemary and status quo

fertilizes the pole beans. Over behind the

barn, dominant paradigms decompose in

the compost pile with coffee grounds and

last night's broccoli stems.

I once stood on a farm, and I'm going back.

Because there was no for or against

only with

I once stood on a farm, and I'm going back.

Because I'm suffering from habitat loss,

and so are you.

I once stood on a farm, and I'm going back.

Because I'm an endangered species,

and so are you.

I once stood on a farm,

and I went back.

Afterall,

    that agricultural situation

        was my existential revelation:

A community!
    In full bloom!
        Tangible,
            possible,
                …edible!

        I saw the Farmer

        in conversation

        living

    at the confluence

      of Humans

      and Nature

        …

And there it was:

an inkling

of an essence

some…

…Thing

existing

ethereal

hidden in the breeze

just

out of reach

begging for the finding

in the intertidal wash

where Nature

bleeds into

Human:

a Presence

gnawing at my own

what

was It?

hmm.

It seems this story

really begins

with a question

"What *is* the relationship

between an ecological farmer

and their farm?"

That's why I went back:

to get the answer.

. . .

How though?

How indeed.

…but first…

What is ecological agriculture?

                              Good question.

In ecological agriculture

vegetables form guilds

and shout

hell no!

to gmo's

pigs left behind

by conquistadors

turn their noses up

at Monsanto's finest

and tomatoes scorn

the latest vintage from Dow Industrial

Didn't you know?

cucumbers disdain

any and all laboratory appellations

in short,

no pesticide applications

or herbicides

...or antibiotics, for that matter

the Farmer as ecologist

doing it the way Nature does it

where the birds and the bees are free

to do,

um,

*cough

as they do.

There is no tilling

so, don't think

rows of corn

or pretty red barns

think bushy

      and wild

But back to how:

using words like
　　revelation
　　　　essence
　　　　　　confluence
　　　　　　　　Heart
　　　　　　　　　and ether
these are not the words
of the realm objective.
besides
who are we kidding?
even at its core
the most objective inquiry
begins in choice
　　　　a subjective choice
　　　　　　to be objective
the path to *fact*
　　　　beginning
　　　　　　in *belief.*

So let's dispense

with the pleasantries

and illusion

light explodes

into fragments of impression

      and symbolic constructions

maelstroms of meaning

      and cultural conditions

once the end of the optic nerve it does

reach.

So, my inquiry

rests comfortable

In the realm subjective

…

oh!

look!

Being!

in Community!

a phenomenon

joined–by–hyphens

(it's really quite phenomenal)

so: phenomenology
that's apropos
and situates me
right in the thick of it
I'm the medium
through which this phenomenon
flows
I'm your access
    head hands and Heart
        a tripartite instrument of inquiry!
            where's my cape?
But!

You can't ask a microscope

        to look at the stars

don't ask a ruler

        to measure the atom;

                of course, it's subjective

I'm the only me

    the only me

        who can see

            what I see

I'm your filter
giving you access
to this phenomenon
and so I communicate it honestly
Authentically
looking out past Ivory Towers
over Ivory Walls
to where the information belongs
in the heads
hands
And Hearts
of The People

Me
in the thick of it
Me
as instrument
Me
as medium
communicating Authentically

Hm. What else?

Research needs tools
participant-driven photo-elicitation
is a good one
and the right one for this research
where the Farmers take pictures
based on a question
but my question?
too nebulous
too broad
too open
Words
I do love Words

how about thirteen of them?
whole, self, cycle,
dialogue, diversity, collaboration
community, empathy, adaptation,
learning, wonder,
spontaneity,
harmony
each a view
into this being-in-community
phenomenon
each a window
into one house
our house
our Home
participant driven photo-elicitation
each Farmer given thirteen Words
to associate with moments
from their daily lives
of which to take pictures
then
once all pictures are taken
all photos sent:

                        interviews
               using those same pictures
                     as backbone
                      on which
                    Conversation
                       is built

                         ...

Me
as Researcher
the Farmers:
lowly participants
          read: subjects
                    read: objects
Ooo
the principles do shudder
But!
the Farmer: the expert on their life
on this phenomenon
of being-in-community

Me: the student

the learner

an ontological inversion!

power cartwheels

phenomenon, Farmer, researcher

  in conversation

     in collaboration

        co–creating

           NEW knowledge

Hey!

a collaborative inquiry

       into collaborative existence

          generating collaboration

             a research hat trick!

But you're here for the findings,
real quick:
writing–as–analysis
I used that
I wrote
jotted
and scribbled
my path into
and through
analyzing the interviews
the head and hands
working together
create greater
Insight
than when they work alone.

Also,

cold emails were sent

in–person

was im–possible

there was a pandemic, you see

many, many,

many, many, many

many, many,

emails

really,

they were legion

five Farms responded

and those five Farmers

made today possible

five Farmers, thirteen Words,

ten videoed interviews

One more thing:

I wanted to breathe the Farms
to smell the flowers,
roses, to be glib,
walk the earth where the Farmers walked
Be
where the Farmers
met Being
my Wife made the travel possible
she found a vehicle of recreation
in the midst of global devastation
today wouldn't be possible.
without her, either

Okay,

Results,

such a vacuous word.

Data!

     Data!

what a laughable thing to call what

happened

Data.

Interviews,

an ontological Rorschach test

shadows and light at play

on the forest floor of my Subconscious

Words, themes,

dominant, secondary

three reflections coalesced

The Self,

Death,

and

Being In Community

no one superior to the other

no one before the other,

(to hell with linear order)

here they are

...as they emerged.

The Self.

The self?

What is self?

Where does self begin?

Where does self

end?

I don't know

Is it my body?

I don't know.

Is it this flesh?

I don't know

Is the self-bound

to a fateful return

by shackles forged of inevitability?

An ephemeral emergence

of inanimate matter

walking, talking

dead matter

thinking and feeling

wondering

"What am I?

until the wind reclaims the ashes

and the dust comes to rest?
Or is there something left behind?
I don't know.
Receding shadows
reveal the self in hiding
A glimpse
An orphan
Fearful
Flees
Cowers
in an overgrown orchard
Just
beyond the brambles
Just
beyond the thorns
Just
out of reach
Where is self?
Where did it go?
I don't know

But I followed it here
To this garden
at our beginning
…
How do you find a self
if you don't know what one looks like?
I don't know
but this is a good place to start:
The self
Not just an embodied self
here interred within a separate there
No…
Not an isolated self
an atomized "I"
psychically exiled
from the ecological "we"
No…
Not an instantiated self
a singular monochromatic snapshot
No…

The Self radiates outward

incorporating others

interwoven with those most dear

A fusion of penumbra

Constant

Persistent across time

The self can be one

The self can be other

The self can be many

The self can be before

It can be yet to come

The self is always

Now

A murmurating constellational interaction

reciprocally intersubjectively

permeating the landscape

in which it finds itself

The self!

An emergent spatial, social

chronological,

simultaneity

…Nebulous

…Esoteric

…Damn.

Would the Farmer still be

without the Farm…?

Would the Farm still be

without the Farmer…?

What does the wind's voice sound like?

In what timbre

does a tree speak?

One

without the other

is silent

So too

The self

invisible

Non-existent

without community

Without the self

Community

disintegrates,

Non-existent.

The self

an atom

a conversational coherence

of constituent parts

whirling

in quantum infinity

bleeding

into raw nature

The Self:

the point at which

humans

and Nature

become one.

Death

    ...*death*

       ...death

There is an intrinsic continuity in death.
It's hard to see when taken out of context
the removal of death from our daily...

               from our culture...

On the farm
where Death

   wanders along the rows

       scythe stained green,

           the continuity

              is glaring

Where rooster

   becomes squash

      and squash rooster

Where offal

    is delectable

        after a season

            in the compost pile

On the Farm

    Death's presence

        is unavoidable

            imperative

Death

    breathes *life*

        into the soil

Imprisoned in finitude

we fail to see

and then believe

that life begins and ends

instead of realizing

Life and Death

are one

    a singular becoming

             in circular unity

Where

    Ends cease to be

Where

    Beginnings end:

            Being,

              in cyclical perpetuity

What is it to us?

        off the Farm

          beyond the Garden Gates

where the delusion

of Death's absence

persists

    through willful ignorance

              and fear?

tick

tick

tick

mechanical

repetitive

persistent

Terror

no matter...

Know!

Conquer!

Culminate!

Ever after!

Once and for all!

for us,

Eternity!

at the expense

of life itself.

The dream of infants

perched,

teetering

atop highchairs

of illusion

weathered

by Death's inexorable

tempering presence

Turn towards Death

Embrace Death

Feel Death

Move through Death

otherwise

we're just Icarus

waiting for our day

in the sun

Babel's Tower

on shaky ground

building,

    building,

        building

          the distance

        between humanity

        and the Earth

          growing,

                growing,

                        growing

Now...

all that remains...

Being in community

the final phenomenon

within the phenomenon

what better place to start?

than with a definition

a point, Archimedean

spiraling outwards, then

towards an articulation

of the process of community

Community, though

elusive

a definition

hard to grasp,

idiomatically speaking

Community:

fluidly dynamic and intersubjective

undulating,

    transcendent

lava lamp interbeing
aorta adjacent sign reads "access only"
blood-pumping, inside-chest organ
four chamber eyes see circles, reciprocals, integrations; corporeally conversationally coherently constitutionally constellational polylectic teleologies of teleologies of teleological teleologies; kaleidoscopic self from self-reflecting in-dwelling self-reflecting selves realizing convivial polycorporeal physiology: final definition semblance reached! clap phenomena in language irons, being in grammar handcuffs syllabic exudate from mind swamp buries Forms of Things things-in-themselves lived experience lost in intellectual neuron forest; phenomena slate wiped clean wisdom drowns in white-capped knowledge waves on word seas...

…My words

    getting in the way

        of *their Lesson*

and so, I stepped aside:

Harmony arises,

nestled within the unity of diversity,

in a polyphony of perspectives.

Abandon knowing.

Open

to the spontaneous,

the unpredictable, the inevitable.

Embrace wonder,

paradox.

Listen.

Learn.

Welcome chaos…

…in the interstices

This is not a story about ecological

agriculture

it's about our relationship

with each other

and the rest of existence

it's about our future

and whether or not we'll have one

About the Author

Raised in South Carolina, educated in Alabama and British Columbia, Walter Cheatham now lives in the swamps of Sanibel Island in Southwest Florida with one existential compass, his wife, and two bedlamites, his children. He is an aspiring contrarian moonlighting as the owner of Anthrogenic Education, LLC which focuses on education consulting and innovative curriculum design and implementation. While Walter has had many roles in his life and though he does on occasion harbor dreams of becoming a raccoon, the roles most important to him are those of husband and father.